FEATHERED FRIENDS

FINCHES

Kim Thompson

NORWOOD HOUSE PRESS

Cataloging-in-Publication Data

Names: Thompson, Kim.
Title: Finches / Kim Thompson.
Description: Buffalo, NY : Norwood House Press, 2027. | Series: Feathered friends | Includes glossary and index.
Identifiers: ISBN 9781978580503 (pbk.) | ISBN 9781978580510 (library bound) | ISBN 9781978580527 (ebook)
Subjects: LCSH: Finches--Juvenile literature.
Classification: LCC QL696.P246 T548 2027 | DDC 598.88--dc23

Published in 2027 by
Norwood House Press
2544 Clinton Street
Buffalo, NY 14224

Designer: Rhea Magaros
Editor: Tricia Hoffman

Photo credits: Cover, p.1 Nataly Studio/Shutterstock.com; p.5 Binson Calfort/Shutterstock.com; p.7 stock images st/Shutterstock.com; p.8 fluffandshutter/Shutterstock.com; p.9 Sari ONeal/Shutterstock.com; p.10 Antonio Gravante/Shutterstock.com; p.11 Bachkova Natalia/Shutterstock.com; p.13 Dmitriy Drozd/Shutterstock.com; p.14 Richard P Long/Shutterstock.com; p.17 noicherrybeans/Shutterstock.com; p.18 Stephen A. Waycott/Shutterstock.com; p.21 Nancy Bauer/Shutterstock.com;

Printed in the United States of America

CPSIA compliance information: Batch #CSNHP27: For further information contact Norwood House Press at 1-800-237-9932.

TABLE OF CONTENTS

What Do Finches Look Like?

Finches are our feathered friends. There are hundreds of finch **species**. The smallest are the length of a playing card. The largest are as long as a piece of printer paper. All finches have cone-shaped **beaks** for cracking seeds.

Many finches have brightly colored feathers. Males are more colorful than females.

House finches have red patches. Purple finches can be raspberry-colored. The American goldfinch is yellow and black.

Where Do Finches Live?

Finches live in warm areas all over the world. They live in North and South America, Europe, and Africa. They like places with shrubs and other low-growing plants. You can find them in parks and backyards.

Finches stay in cold areas during winter as long as they can find seeds to eat. Farmers like finches because they eat the seeds of unwanted weeds.

How Do Finches Grow Up?

Finches build cup-shaped nests on the ground, in bushes, or in trees. Nests are made of twigs, grass, and roots. Females lay four or five eggs at a time.

Eggs **hatch** in about two weeks. In most species, both the mother and the father care for chicks. Babies leave the nest two or three weeks after they hatch.

Finches are very **social**. They fly in **flocks**. They are often seen flying along with birds of other species.

What Do Finches Eat?

Finches eat seeds, buds, and berries. They often visit bird feeders. Some finches also eat insects. House finches feed soft fly **larvae** to their chicks.

What Sounds Do Finches Make?

Finches sing to talk to each other. Their cheerful songs have fast twitters, **warbles**, and whistles. American goldfinches seem to call out, “po-ta-to-chip, po-ta-to-chip.”

Some finches **mimic** the songs of other birds. When the lesser goldfinch sings, it includes sounds copied from wrens and robins.

What Funny Things Can Finches Do?

Finches will do anything to find tasty seeds. Some hang upside down on plants to find their favorite foods.

GLOSSARY

beaks (beeks): horny, pointed jaws on birds; bird bills

flocks (flahks): groups of animals of one kind that live, travel, or feed together

hatch (hach): to break out of an egg to be born

larvae (LAHR-vee): insects at a stage of development after they hatch from eggs, when they look like worms

mimic (MIM-ik): to imitate someone else; to copy

social (SOH-shuhl): preferring to be with others instead of alone

species (SPEE-sheez): groups of living things that are alike and can reproduce together

warbles (WAHR-buhls): series of pleasing, back-and-forth musical notes

THINKING QUESTIONS

1. How big are finches?

2. Name two types of finches.

3. Why do farmers like finches?

4. What do finches eat?

5. Describe finch songs.

INDEX

ABOUT THE AUTHOR

Kim Thompson is a writer from Columbus, Ohio. She has written many books for kids. Lots of birds come to her backyard feeder. Her favorites are the showy red cardinals, tiny bright goldfinches, and waddling mallard ducks. Her two cats watch from the window.